Disaster Zone

The Science Behind RAGING WILDFIRES

Louise Spilsbury

CHERITON
CHILDREN'S BOOKS

Please visit our website, www.cheritonchildrensbooks.com to see more of our high-quality books.

First Edition

Published in 2022 by **Cheriton Children's Books**
PO Box 7258, Bridgnorth WV16 9ET, UK

Author: Louise Spilsbury
Designer: Paul Myerscough
Editor: Tim Cooke
Proofreader: Wendy Scavuzzo
Picture Researcher: Rachel Blount
Consultant: David Hawksett, BSc

Picture credits: Cover: Shutterstock/Christian Roberts-Olsen; Inside: p1: Shutterstock/Joseph Sohm; pp4-5: Shutterstock/Christian Roberts-Olsen; p5r: Shutterstock/Erin Donalson; p6: Shutterstock; p7: Shutterstock/Anna LoFi; p8: Shutterstock/Joseph Sohm; p9: Shutterstock/Michael Neil Thomas; pp10-11: Wikimedia Commons/NASA (Joshua Stevens); p11c: Shutterstock/Dylan Mittag; pp12-13: Shutterstock; p13b: Shutterstock/Neil Lockhart; p14: Shutterstock/Soloviova Liudmyla; p15: Shutterstock/Aresubb; p16: Shutterstock/Alin Brotea; p17: Shutterstock/Totajla; pp18-19: Wikimedia Commons/Daniel Cleaveley; p19b: Wikimedia Commons/Nick Pitsas, CSIRO; pp20-21: Shutterstock/Yelantsevv; p21r: Shutterstock/JOEYSTUDIO; p22: Shutterstock/Itsajoop; p23: Wikimedia Commons/Self; p24: Shutterstock/VanderWolf Images; p25: Shutterstock/Mikeledray; pp26-27: Shutterstock; p27b: Shutterstock/GUDKOV ANDREY; pp28-29: Shutterstock/FCG; p29t: Shutterstock/Morphius Film; p30: Shutterstock/Epixproductions; p31: NASA/METI/AIST/Japan Space Systems, and U.S./Japan ASTER Science Team; pp32-33: Shutterstock/StoneWolf24; p33t: Shutterstock/Eugene R Thieszen; pp34-35: Shutterstock/Denis Belitsky; p35r: Wikimedia Commons/Martin Olsson; p36: Shutterstock/StockPhotosLV; p37: Shutterstock/TFoxFoto; pp38-39: Shutterstock/Bruno Ismael Silva Alves; p38b: Shutterstock/StacieStauffSmith Photos; pp40-41: Shutterstock/Tsomka; pp40-41b: Shutterstock/Ronstik; p42: Shutterstock/ARM Photo Video; p43: Shutterstock/Photka; p44: Shutterstock/Brendt A Petersen; p45: U.S. Department of Defense/Marine Corps photo by Cpl. Lukas Kalinauskas; p47: Shutterstock/Alin Brotea.

Printed in the United States of America

Contents

Chapter 1

MEGA BLAZES

A wildfire is when a natural area, such as a forest, **grassland**, or **prairie**, catches fire and flames then spread quickly and out of control over a wide region. The worst of these blazes can cause terrible damage to plants and wildlife, property, and people.

Fires Under Control

Sometimes, people set fire to particular parts of wild places on purpose. That is because some new or young plants grow better in these burned areas. The burned areas are also good for **grazing livestock**, and cleared areas of land can provide more open **habitat** for rare animals such as Florida panthers, too. People start these fires for a purpose and put them out before they cause damage to the **environment** and its animals. These types of fire are not wildfires because they are controlled.

Wildfires can blaze through an area of forest quickly. They light up the sky and fill the air with the sound of snapping and crackling as trees are destroyed.

Fires Out of Control

Wildfires start and spread in an **unpredictable** and entirely uncontrolled way. Some wildfires are small and firefighters can put them out before they cause a lot of damage. Large forest fires, however, move and spread quickly. They destroy everything in their path. They can make trees explode and can hurl balls of fire into the air. Most people escape these fires, but some are injured or killed by the smoke, flames, or falling trees.

Wildfires can burn for days or weeks, destroying everything in their paths before they are brought under control.

MEGA WILDFIRES

Megafires are wildfires that burn more than 100,000 acres (40,470 ha). Megafires are the biggest, fastest-moving fires imaginable. A small fire can reach temperatures twice as hot as an average pizza oven. However, a megafire in a tall forest can create flames 150 feet (46 m) high that are one-quarter of the temperature of the sun's surface. Megafires are unstoppable. They devour towns and cities. They explode entire houses. Their flames, heat, and choking smoke can kill many people.

DEADLY DISASTERS

Wildfires are called forest fires, grassland fires, or **bushfires**, depending on the types of plants being burned by the flames. Whatever their name, these fires scorch the earth. They destroy plants and leave animals homeless.

Forests in Flame

One of the most destructive forms of wildfires happens in forests. If one tree catches fire in a forest, it warms the air and the trees nearby. Then those trees catch fire, too. Forests contain thousands of trees close together. Soon, enormous areas can be burning at the same time. However, fire can spread through a forest even if the trees are not close together. Flames are spread by smaller plants that grow below or among the trees. Dry leaves, twigs, branches, and other materials on the forest floor also spread fire.

Fires can spread from tree to tree quickly, until very soon an entire forest is ablaze.

Wildlife Under Attack

Fires can be a disaster. They affect not only the trees and plants in a forest, grassland, or other wild place, but also the animals that live there. Some animals, such as birds and deer, may be able to fly from or outrun the flames. Other animals, from snakes to livestock kept in fields, may be burned alive. Animals that escape the fire may not be able to survive for much longer. If a wildfire destroys the habitat where they lived, their home is destroyed. The land can no longer provide them with shelter from bad weather. It can't protect them from **predators** or provide the food, such as leaves, bark, fruit, and nuts, which they need to eat. Some animals, including orangutans and tree kangaroos, are in danger of **extinction** because of habitat loss. Wildfires are one of the main reasons for habitat loss.

Q: Why do you think predators are more of a threat to animals that have lost their habitat?

The animals that do survive wildfires in Australia, such as this kangaroo, are left trying to survive in a habitat destroyed by the flames.

Where in the World?

In 2009, millions of animals, including kangaroos, wombats, birds, reptiles, and pets, were killed in wildfires that destroyed more than 1.1 million acres (445,154 ha) in Victoria, Australia. Even birds and bats did not escape—the extreme heat killed them, too. They fell from the sky, dead.

A TRAIL OF DESTRUCTION

Large wildfires leave a trail of destruction behind them. As well as wiping out large areas of plants and animals, wildfires cost countries millions of dollars. It is expensive to fight fires. Cleaning up after them, and rebuilding houses and buildings destroyed by flames costs a lot of money.

Reaching Towns and Cities

Wildfires can destroy homes and buildings within a forest or other natural area. They can also spread so far and fast that they reach the outskirts of towns and cities. They will start to burn buildings there, too. The flames quickly burn down homes, schools, and other buildings. These structures become more **fuel** for the fire. The fires can melt roads, and bend bridges. They can explode fuel at gas stations and in damaged pipes. The intense heat can shatter glass and crumble bricks. Entire walls will then collapse.

These homes were destroyed by deadly wildfires that spread into Ventura, California, in 2018.

Fire Deaths

Some people are killed when they are trapped by flames from a wildfire. Others die when they try to escape a burning forest, or the fire spreads to the buildings where they are. However, it is not just flames that kill—the smoke from wildfires is equally destructive. A wildfire can fill the air with smoke, which contains poisonous gases and **particles**. It also contains tiny jagged pieces of unburned material called **particulate matter**. When people breathe that in, it gets inside their lungs and makes breathing very difficult. The particles can also travel out of the lungs and damage other body parts, such as the heart.

Charred Remains

After a wildfire dies out, it leaves behind a **charred** and blackened landscape. Everything is covered in dirty, dusty ash. It is very difficult to clean up in towns and cities, and forests and farmland can be ruined. Soils are rich in nutrients, or natural substances that help trees and other plants grow. Many living things live in soil, including earthworms. They help keep it healthy. The intense heat from large wildfires can destroy the living things that make soil **fertile**. That makes it difficult for some trees and plants to grow on the land for a very long time.

This trail of destruction was left by a devastating forest fire in northern California. It was caused by lightning strikes after very dry weather.

WILDFIRE POLLUTION

Around the world each year, wildfires release around 2 million tons (1.8 million mt) of particulate matter into Earth's **atmosphere**. That is more than the pollution that comes from vehicles and factories.

California

The Camp Fire in the northern California foothills started on November 8, 2018. The region's fire season should have been almost over, however, a long period without rain meant that plant life was dry and easily caught fire.

Fire Starter

At 6:43 a.m., firefighters arrived near Camp Creek in the Sierra Nevada foothills to check on a fire below some power lines near the Poe Dam. They realized they were watching the start of a wildfire. The winds were then 35 miles per hour (56 kph). Later that day, they whipped up to 70 miles per hour (113 kph). The winds fanned the flames down the Feather River Canyon, toward the small towns at its base.

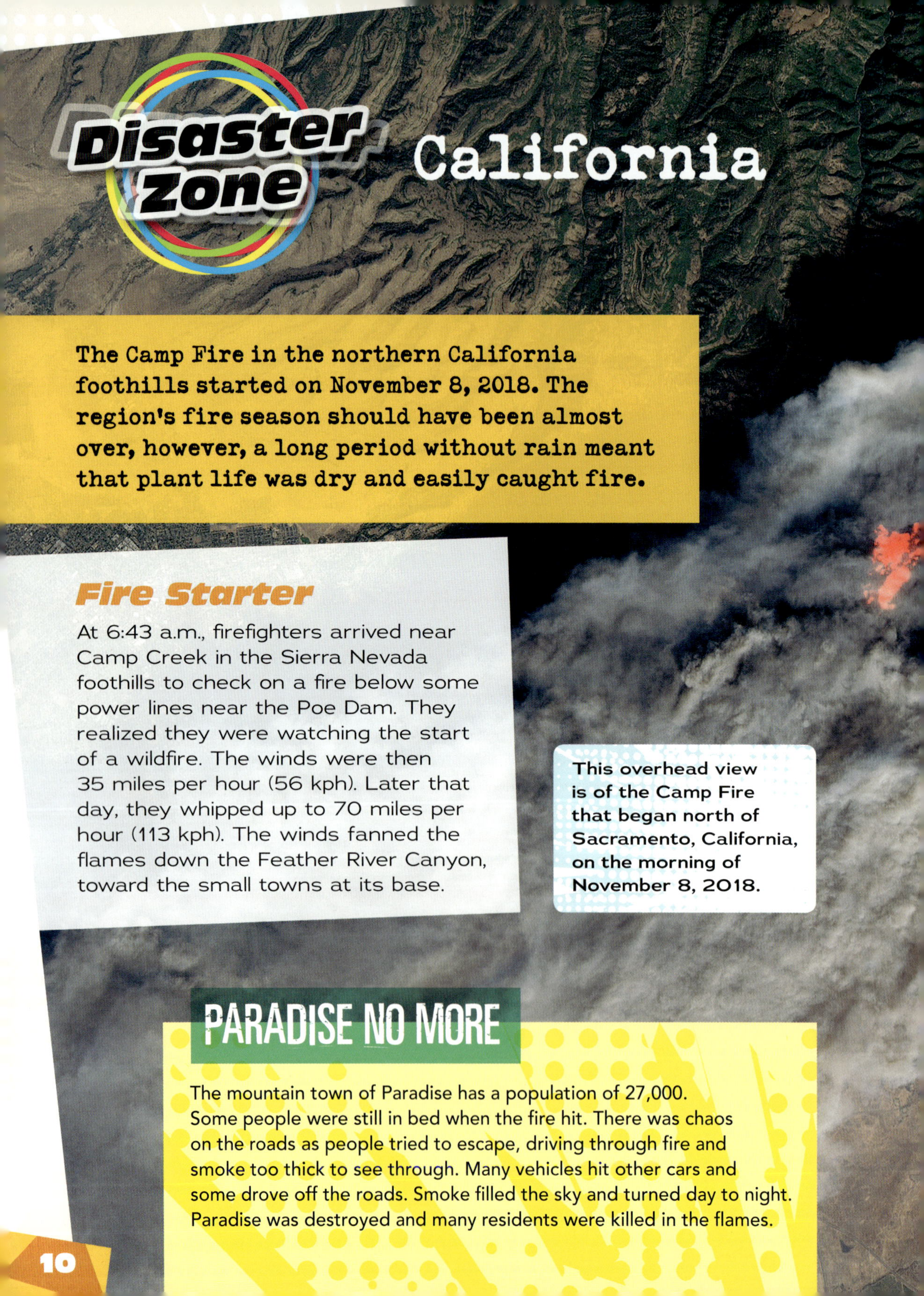

This overhead view is of the Camp Fire that began north of Sacramento, California, on the morning of November 8, 2018.

PARADISE NO MORE

The mountain town of Paradise has a population of 27,000. Some people were still in bed when the fire hit. There was chaos on the roads as people tried to escape, driving through fire and smoke too thick to see through. Many vehicles hit other cars and some drove off the roads. Smoke filled the sky and turned day to night. Paradise was destroyed and many residents were killed in the flames.

Everything Ablaze

The fire grew rapidly in just a few hours. By around midday, the fire had burned 10,000 acres (4,047 ha) in about 90 minutes. That's more than one football field every second! In its first day alone, the wildfire burned more than 70,000 acres (28,330 ha) of land. As it tore through Butte County, thousands of people in the region had to leave, including those from schools and hospitals. Some people were forced to leave their vehicles and escape on foot. Emergency crews worked hard to rescue residents trapped in their homes.

The deadly fire was finally declared to be over after 17 days of burning, on November 25, 2018. It left 85 people dead and at least 17 people injured. The deadly fire had covered an area of almost 153,600 acres (62,160 ha) and destroyed almost 19,000 buildings.

Drivers in Paradise said black smoke and red flames were all that they could see.

Q The Camp fire caused terrible physical devastation. What emotional effects do you think it may have had on its victims?

Chapter 2

HOW WILDFIRES WORK

Whether a wildfire is big or small, it can only happen where there is **oxygen**, fuel, and heat. These three things are the corners of what is known as the fire triangle. The biggest wildfires in the world have a lot of each of these ingredients.

Once a wildfire starts, it does not only burn plants. It burns any other fuel it can find, too, including homes and other buildings.

Ingredients for a Wildfire

Flames start when oxygen, which is a gas found in the air, mixes with anything that can burn. That is the fuel. Fuel includes any material that can catch fire, such as trees, grasses, **brush**, and buildings. Burning is a **chemical reaction**. It can happen only when there is enough heat. Wildfires start when plants or trees are heated to a temperature at which they are hot enough to catch fire, or burst into flames. Wood catches fire when it reaches a temperature of 570 degrees Fahrenheit (300 °C). This temperature is known as its flash point. When wood reaches its flash point, gases released from the wood react with oxygen. That produces flames.

Starting a Wildfire

Wildfires can start in different ways. Sometimes, nature starts the fire. Some wildfires begin when lightning strikes. Lightning bolts can be very hot. When they hit dry plants, they create a spark of heat that can start a fire.

Some wildfires are caused by volcanoes. Volcanoes can spit out super-hot clouds of ash. They also spit out hot, liquid rock, called lava. Lava and ash can easily set trees on fire and start wildfires. When a fire has started, its flames heat up fuels nearby. That helps the fire grow and easily spread.

FUELING WILDFIRES

Wildfires in forests and prairies spread easily once they start. That's because there is a lot of fuel in the form of wood, leaves, and brush. There is also a lot of oxygen. Plants release oxygen into the air as they make their own food inside their leaves. That process is called photosynthesis.

When lightning sets a small area of dry grass on fire, the fire heats the plants around it even more, so sparks set these plants alight, too.

FATAL SPARKS

Some wildfires are started by natural causes. However, most wildfires are the result of human activity. Either on purpose or by accident, people often create the sparks that cause the worst wildfire blazes.

Human Causes

People can spark wildfires in many ways. For example, arson is when someone starts a fire on purpose to cause trouble. However, more often, fires start because of carelessness. A wildfire can start when people don't put out a campfire or bonfire before leaving it. Other fires start when a driver flicks a lit cigarette out of the car window when driving through a natural area. Fireworks set off near a wild area could also start a wildfire if not handled properly. Some wildfires are the result of farming called slash-and-burn. Farmers cut down trees and then light small fires to clear the remaining stumps and waste wood. The farmers want to plant **crops** or keep livestock there. Those fires can accidentally spread to surrounding trees. They can get out of control, creating a dangerous wildfire.

A campfire is a great part of camping, but campers should always watch the fire and put it out carefully to prevent a wildfire from starting.

Where in the World?

On July 22, 2012, in Catalonia, Spain, a wildfire broke out that covered almost 35,000 acres (14,164 ha) of land. It also killed two people. They tried to escape the flames by jumping from cliffs into the sea. Investigators discovered that the fire was caused by a cigarette not being properly put out. At the edge of a road in the area, forest rangers found hundreds of cigarette butts.

This photograph shows the destruction caused by the 2012 wildfire in Catalonia.

Happening by Accident

Wildfires can happen entirely by accident. Electrical machinery and power lines can produce electrical sparks. They can act like tiny lightning bolts and start fires. A running engine can spit out hot sparks when there is something wrong. Car crashes have also been known to start fires quickly. One forest fire happened when someone hammered a fence post into dirt among dry plants. The sparks set off a blaze. Wind can fan small fires, making them bigger and causing them to spread at high speed. Wind can blow sparks or **embers** onto new plants, starting new fires.

Q

How would you educate people about the dangers of starting a wildfire, either accidentally or on purpose? How would you persuade them to change their behaviors?

HOW WILDFIRES SPREAD

Once a fire is lit, it quickly creates a huge amount of heat and **energy** that can make it spread fast and far. A wildfire can rapidly swallow up all the wood, plants, and trees in its path.

Wind-Powered Fury

Fires can create their own winds because they keep heating up the air above the ground. As the air warms, it rises. Then, as cooler air blows in to take its place, that movement of air creates winds. The winds created by the terrible heat push hot air ahead of them. That can send sparks and embers hundreds of feet ahead of the fire. The heated air and those sparks and embers can set trees and homes on fire. They start new fires even before the **original** wall of flames has reached an area.

A large, aggressive fire that spreads by its own winds and fireballs is called a conflagration.

Blasting Fireballs

Some fires spread not as a solid wall of flame, but from the treetops. Fire can easily set ablaze the thin stems of climbing plants such as vines and ivy. These plants grow tall by clinging onto tree trunks, and when the plants catch fire, the flames spread up their stems. The flames then quickly catch onto the leafy top of the tree, which is called the crown. Crown fires spread fast through a forest, because the flames pass from crown to crown. Fast-rising winds can also blow burning embers from a crown high into the air, creating fireballs. Those fireballs can burn for up to six minutes in the air. They can travel for thousands of feet. When fireballs land in a tree ahead of the main flames, they start new crown fires.

FIRE WHIRLS

A fire whirl is a whirlwind of flame or ash. It happens when an area of wildfire is whipped straight upward by strong, dry air. Fire whirls can reach more than 1,000 feet (305 m) tall and last for more than 20 minutes. Their temperatures can be hotter than 2,000 degrees Fahrenheit (1,093 °C)! Fire whirls can uproot trees and can send burning embers far into the air. That spreads fires farther and more quickly.

Fire whirls are also known as fire devils.

Disaster Zone

Victoria, Australia

On February 7, 2009, a series of bushfires raged across the state of Victoria in Australia. Those fierce and incredibly hot fires were deadly and destructive. The day when they began became known as Black Saturday.

The Black Saturday fires were so intense that they created huge columns of flames that burned everything in their paths.

Feeling the Heat

The summer of 2009 had seen record-breaking temperatures of up to 115 degrees Fahrenheit (46 °C) in Victoria. That heatwave had dried up the land and plants in the region, so they were much more likely to catch fire. On February 7, fast winds knocked down power lines and created sparks. They lit the first flames. As the day continued, the wildfire grew and spread. The fire created winds of 75 miles per hour (120 kph). They blew huge fireballs, which spread the wildfire quickly through trees and towns. Spot fires sprang up miles downwind of the main fire. By the evening of February 7, there were almost 400 separate fires burning.

Fearsome Flames

The fires joined together and became a gigantic bushfire. The flames were so hot that they melted metal. They leaped 70 feet (20 m) into the air, sending up columns of smoke thousands of feet tall. Some people tried to escape the fires by car, but the flames were too fast to outpace. Many people died on the roads in flames or in collisions as they tried to speed to safety. In total, the fires that struck Victoria in 2009 killed more than 1 million animals. About 1.1 million acres (445,154 ha) of land was burned. The fires injured 414 people, killed 173, and left more than 7,500 homeless.

SAVED BY THE WEATHER

Thousands of firefighters battled the fires for days. They tried to stop them from spreading by clearing their fuel. They cut down trees and plants in the flames' path and sprayed flames with water. One of the people who died in the fire was a firefighter. He was crushed by a falling tree. The Black Saturday fires continued until March 14 when the weather changed. With less fuel and the hard work of firefighters, the flames were finally put out.

The fires killed many people who tried to escape them by car. This burned-out car was found at Kinglake, a town in Victoria, after the Black Saturday bushfires.

Chapter 3

WHERE RAGING WILDFIRES HAPPEN

Wildfires can happen anywhere there is an area of plants that can catch fire and burn easily. Once a wildfire starts to burn, it can either fizzle out or grow into a raging blaze. It depends partly on what type of fuel is available and how much of it there is.

Types of Fuel

Some types of plants or trees catch fire and burn more easily than others. For example, coniferous trees have needles all year round. They usually burn faster than deciduous trees, which have flat leaves that drop off in fall. That is because the branches of coniferous trees contain large amounts of a sticky substance called resin, which easily catches fire. Eucalyptus trees burn faster and hotter than many other trees. Both their sap and bark catch fire easily. The bark flies off when it is burned, starting new fires.

A tree is big and thick so it takes time to catch fire. Thin twigs, dry blades of grass and leaves, dry cones, and pine needles burst into flame much more readily.

Where in the World?

In 2017, Chile's worst-ever wildfires killed 11 people. They burned about 1.3 million acres (518,000 ha), and destroyed settlements. The fires burned out of control because a lot of eucalyptus trees were planted close together. The trees had been planted to be later sold as wood. The tightly packed trees burned rapidly and spread the flames easily.

Eucalyptus trees, like the ones shown right, fueled the 2017 wildfires in Chile.

Fuel Load

The fuel load is the amount of fuel, including wood, dry plants, and brush, per area of ground surrounding a fire. Forests burn more slowly when there is a smaller fuel load than with a bigger one. Not all the fuel load is above ground. Some of the fuel load that burns is below the ground. Roots, dead wood, plant waste, and some types of soil burn well, too. If a lot of trees in a forest have been cut down, the fuel load is spaced out and fires tend to slow down. Coniferous trees generally grow closer together than deciduous trees, and fire spreads more easily and faster between them. Fires slow down or stop when they reach places such as rivers and wide roads, and they run out of fuel load.

WILDFIRES AND THE WEATHER

Wildfires do not usually happen when it is cold, wet, or snowy. Most wildfires begin during a heatwave or after a long period of hot, dry weather. Fires are made worse and spread more easily when it is very windy.

Hot and Dry

Wildfires spread faster when plants are drier. If trees and plants contain a lot of moisture, that slows down fires. That is why people pour water on a campfire to put it out. After rain, plants, trees, and **debris** on a forest floor are too damp to catch fire. In drier, warmer seasons of the year and in places with dry **climates**, there is a lot more fuel for fires to burn. Drought is a very long period without any rain. It makes the land and plants extra dry. This means they will catch fire much more easily if touched by a spark.

Hot sun and dry weather has made this meadow grass in Extremadura, Spain, highly **flammable**, creating an extreme risk of wildfire.

Where in the World?

The people who died in the 1871 Peshtigo Fire are remembered in the memorial at the Peshtigo Fire Cemetery.

The Peshtigo Fire of October 1871 in Wisconsin was the worst wildfire recorded in American history. It had been a long, very dry summer and fall. The conditions were just right for a large, rapidly spreading fire. Large piles of sawdust and wood waste from cutting trees helped fires spread quickly through the forest. The fires created fast winds. They ripped up trees, blew roofs off buildings, and blasted apart barns. Around 2,400 people died in the fire. More than 1.2 million acres (485,620 ha) of forest was burned to the ground. For many years after the fire, the ruined land was unable to support any form of life.

Whipped Up by Winds

Wind can be caused by changes in the weather or by a wildfire. The wind increases the flow of oxygen to more of the plants near a fire. It makes the flames spread faster and speeds up the movement of fires across the land. The wind also increases the rate at which water **evaporates** from plants near an approaching fire. That means the plants are drier and will catch fire more easily.

PLACES AT RISK

Wildfires can happen anywhere. However, they are most likely in places with particular types of climates. They are also more likely to happen in some seasons than in others. Those are known as fire seasons.

Wildfire-Friendly Climates

Wildfire-friendly climates are climates that make wildfires more possible. They are found in places that get enough rain to allow a lot of plants and trees to grow. Those places also have long hot, dry periods during which plants dry out and become more likely to catch fire. Wildfires are common in forest regions of Canada and the United States. They also happen in areas such as the grasslands of Australia. The forests and grasslands of the Western Cape of South Africa are other wildfire-friendly places. There is no limit to where wildfires can happen. They have happened in places as far apart as Greece and the Arctic Circle.

Places with long hot seasons are most at risk of devastating wildfires.

Fire Seasons

Different countries and different areas of countries experience the worst conditions for wildfires at different times of the year. **Tropical** countries, such as India, have only a rainy and a dry season. There, the typical fire season is from January to June, when it is dry. After that, heavy **monsoon** rains put out any fires. In a country such as the United States, there are four seasons. Wildfires are more likely in summer, when the heat makes fuels drier, or in the fall. Then, dead branches, leaves, and other material are fully dried out and highly flammable. California has two fire seasons: the summer season and the Santa Ana season in fall, when hot, dry winds blow from inland toward the coast, spreading fires.

Firefighters rush to control fires in California at the end of the fall fire season of 2015. California's Santa Ana winds make parts of the state perfect for wildfires.

THE SANTA ANA WINDS

The Santa Ana winds increase the risk of wildfires. These winds usually blow in southern California and northern Baja California during fall and early winter. In southern California, the Santa Ana winds can help wildfires travel up to 40 miles (64 km) in a single day. They can swallow up to 1,000 acres (405 ha) of land per hour as they rage across the region. The winds blow thick clouds of burning embers ahead of the main fire. That spreads the flames farther.

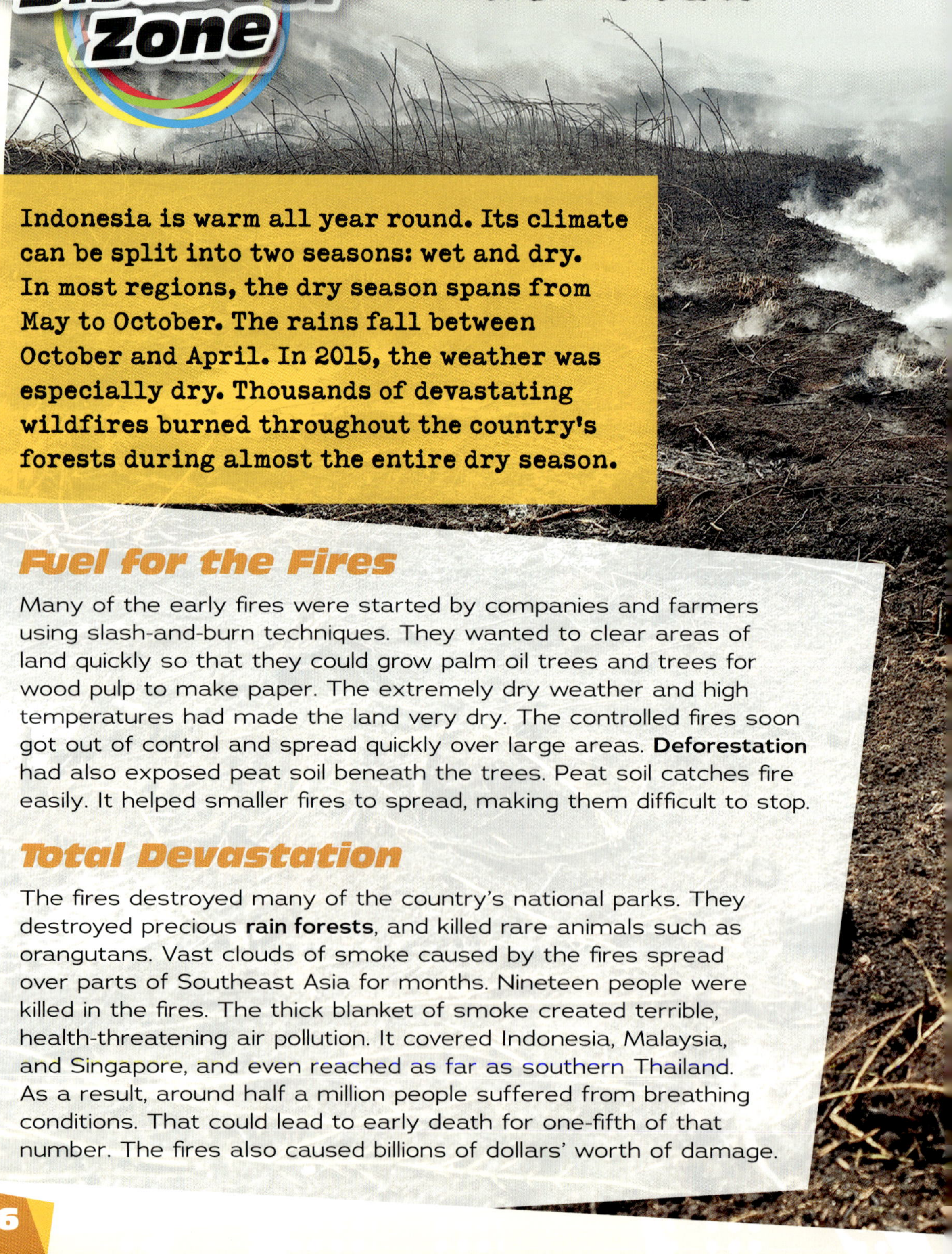

Disaster Zone

Indonesia

Indonesia is warm all year round. Its climate can be split into two seasons: wet and dry. In most regions, the dry season spans from May to October. The rains fall between October and April. In 2015, the weather was especially dry. Thousands of devastating wildfires burned throughout the country's forests during almost the entire dry season.

Fuel for the Fires

Many of the early fires were started by companies and farmers using slash-and-burn techniques. They wanted to clear areas of land quickly so that they could grow palm oil trees and trees for wood pulp to make paper. The extremely dry weather and high temperatures had made the land very dry. The controlled fires soon got out of control and spread quickly over large areas. **Deforestation** had also exposed peat soil beneath the trees. Peat soil catches fire easily. It helped smaller fires to spread, making them difficult to stop.

Total Devastation

The fires destroyed many of the country's national parks. They destroyed precious **rain forests**, and killed rare animals such as orangutans. Vast clouds of smoke caused by the fires spread over parts of Southeast Asia for months. Nineteen people were killed in the fires. The thick blanket of smoke created terrible, health-threatening air pollution. It covered Indonesia, Malaysia, and Singapore, and even reached as far as southern Thailand. As a result, around half a million people suffered from breathing conditions. That could lead to early death for one-fifth of that number. The fires also caused billions of dollars' worth of damage.

POWERFUL PEAT FIRES

Peat is a type of soil made from partly rotted plants. When peat dries out, it burns easily. A peat fire can burn for days or weeks. It can even burn slowly underground and later appear in a different place. These factors make peat fires incredibly difficult to control and put out. They are also hard to predict.

Peat soils that had dried out when exposed to the air by deforestation meant the Indonesian wildfires had a huge supply of fuel.

Heat and smoke drove orangutans out of their forest homes, making it difficult for them to find food and putting them in danger from hunters.

Chapter 4

SCIENTISTS ON THE CASE

The earlier a wildfire can be spotted, the less damage it will cause. With early warning, people can escape from an area before the fire reaches them. That is why scientists are working hard to predict when and where wildfires will happen and to find ways to stop them.

Watching the Weather

Fires happen when it is hot and dry. They spread with the wind. Fire experts study weather forecasts and use **satellite** images. They do so to figure out where thunderstorms might spark a fire and where hot temperatures, low **humidity**, and high winds create fire risks. When a fire starts, they study wind direction to figure out where the fire might go next. That helps them give warnings to people to leave before the flames arrive.

Looking at the Land

Scientists also study the type of land in places where the weather increases the risk of fire. One reason for this is to assess the fuel load. For example, they check if the soil is peat or if there is a lot of dead, dry plant material. These factors mean that any fires in these conditions would spread faster and would also be bigger. Scientists study the slope of the land because fires usually travel uphill much faster than downhill. That is because hot air rises, so flames can more easily reach and burn trees ahead of them uphill than they can on level ground.

These firefighters are dealing with the devastation of the fire that spread uphill at Woolsey California, in 2018.

Knowing what direction the wind is blowing helps scientists figure out where a wildfire is heading next.

EL NIÑO

Scientists also study El Niño events. El Niño is a warm ocean **current** found in the Pacific Ocean. It can cause extreme weather events around the world, roughly every two to seven years. El Niño events happen when the ocean current shifts position around the **equator**. It makes some places wetter and others much hotter than usual. These changes can cause droughts, which increase the risk of wildfires. The 2015 Indonesian fire season was linked to an El Niño drought.

STUDYING VIOLENT INFERNOS

Wildfires start in **remote** places. They are often far from roads or in the center of a thick forest. The best way to spot and learn about big fires is from the air above.

The View from Above

Airplanes, helicopters, and **drones** fly over forests during fire seasons. Infrared cameras onboard these aircraft take a lot of photos at certain places. Infrared is a form of light that we cannot see. However, it can be seen by the heat that it gives off. By comparing the photos, computer programs can spot changes in the amount of heat given off by different parts of a forest. More heat means a higher risk of fire.

Satellites in Space

Wildfires can also be spotted using sensors on weather satellites in space. Satellites examine Earth's surface by watching it from above. A transmitter sends images and information to receivers and computers on Earth. Some weather satellites stay at the same point above Earth. That helps scientists studying the images to spot any changes to the weather at those places. Other satellites circle over the North Pole to the South Pole and back again. They can travel as close to the surface as 160 miles (257 km). They take very detailed pictures of weather patterns all over the world.

Overhead photographs like this one show scientists the extent of damage after a wildfire has blazed through an area.

The dark-colored sections on this satellite image show the area burned by California's Thomas Fire of 2018.

Satellite Sensors

Different satellites and **sensors** scan different parts of wildfires. Like a camera, satellites can take pictures of what they see. They can also make images of things we cannot see with our eyes. Satellite sensors can identify areas that are dry and likely to catch fire. They can show flames or smoldering fires, and areas of land already burned. They can even detect moisture or other changes in the air that can be caused by smoke.

DAY AND NIGHT

One type of satellite can measure the reflected, or bounced back, light and heat given off by Earth. It can find smoke plumes from fires, spot the remains of fires (called burn scars), and active fires. Its ability to find fires is greater at night. During the day, the system can confuse active fires with hot ground, such as sand on the beach.

Disaster Zone

Oklahoma

The Rhea Fire in Dewey County, Oklahoma, began to tear through the Oklahoma Plains on April 12, 2018. A megafire is one that has burned at least 100,000 acres (40,470 ha). The Rhea fire burned 286,196 acres (115,820 ha).

Megafire in the Making

It was wetter than usual in Oklahoma during the summers of 2016 and 2017. That helped a lot of plants grow. Then, in 2018, there was a drought in the area. In some places, it was the driest six months on record. By March 2018, the fire risk was extreme. Strong winds are common across the plains during spring. Those winds helped small fires become a huge damaging fire. The cause of the initial spark was unknown. However, soon flames were swallowing up all of the dried-out grasses in their path and jumping across roads. The blaze turned into Oklahoma's third megafire in three years.

Disaster and Damage

Sparks for the Rhea Fire probably came from human activities. Today, more people live on the edges of wild lands. That increases the chances of people starting fires. It also increases the risk of people being hurt by wildfires. Hundreds of people were forced to leave their homes. At least nine people were injured and two people died. The first victim, a woman, was found dead in her car. A second victim died from injuries he suffered in the fire. More than 50 homes were destroyed and many other buildings, including farms, were also devastated.

Firefighting helicopters dropped water onto the Rhea wildfire in an attempt to control it.

The megafire was known as the Rhea Fire because it started half a mile west of Rhea, Oklahoma.

INCREASING THE THREAT

Unfortunately, people in the Rhea area had also created a buildup of fuels that are most likely to catch fire during dry spells. As well as tall grass and brush, the fuels that kept the Rhea fire burning so violently included the conifer tree red cedar. Red cedar trees had been planted to protect fields of crops in the Rhea area from fierce weather. Red cedar burns hotter and longer than prairie grasses and helped stoke the fires.

Chapter 5

RAGING WILDFIRES OF THE FUTURE

It is likely that there will be more large, fast-moving, and dangerous wildfires in the future. Those megafires will threaten both human lives and the natural world. Many experts believe that climate change increases the risk of more megafires. Many human activities contribute to climate change and increase the risk of wildfires.

What Is Climate Change?

Climate change is a term that describes the way world temperatures have risen. They have risen more quickly in the past 140 years than at any other time in the past 1,400 years. A great majority of scientists believe that climate change is happening now. **Fossil fuels** power factories and machines, and make electricity. When people burn fossil fuels, such as coal, oil, and natural gas, gases are released. Gases such as carbon dioxide will stay in the atmosphere. These gases are known as greenhouse gases. They store heat from the sun, gradually warming the planet.

More Wildfires

The warmer temperatures that come with climate change are changing weather around the world. For example, some places have much longer droughts, which dry out plants and make them more likely to catch fire. That leads to more wildfires. Today, for example, California's fire season is 78 days longer than it was in the 1970s. The region is having drier winters, warmer springs, and hotter summers. Higher temperatures mean more thunderstorms and lightning strikes. Lightning strikes have started many more recent fires in California.

FEARS OF FEEDBACK

Wildfires can make more wildfires because of feedback. Feedback describes changes that lead to more climate change. Plants take in carbon dioxide to make food during the process of photosynthesis. Wildfires destroy trees and plants, which reduces the amount of carbon dioxide being removed from the atmosphere. It then builds up and stores more heat. Plants also release stored carbon dioxide when they burn in wildfires. That adds to climate change and makes more wildfires likely.

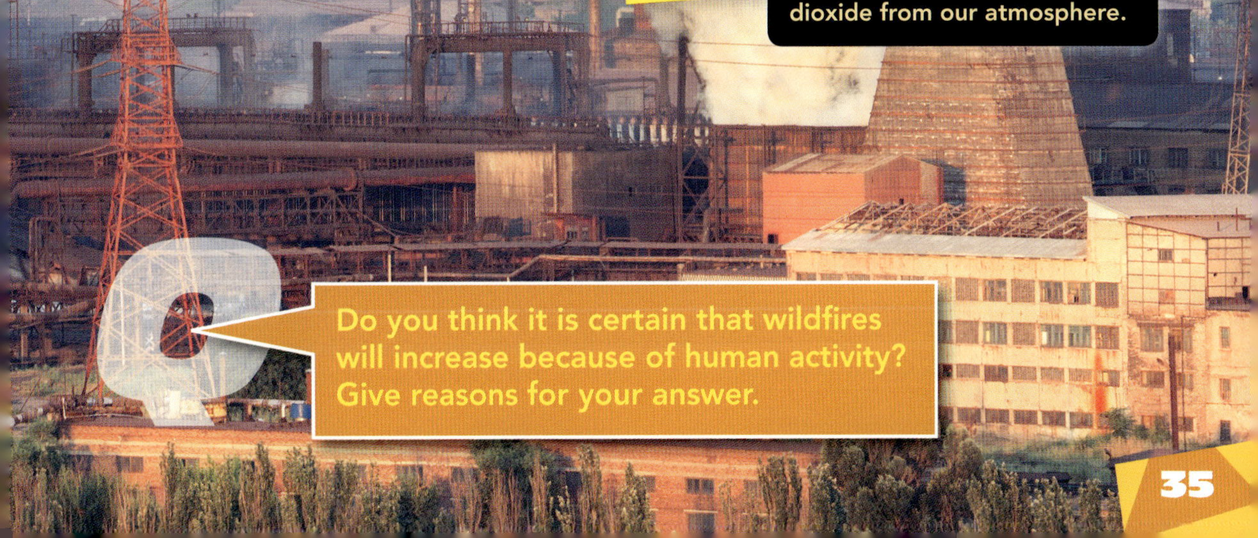

Fossil fuels are burned in factories like this one. This activity is increasing climate change and the risk of wildfires.

Wildfires destroy trees, which we rely on to remove carbon dioxide from our atmosphere.

Q Do you think it is certain that wildfires will increase because of human activity? Give reasons for your answer.

FIGHTING FUTURE WILDFIRES

The increased risk of wildfires and mega blazes in the future means it is more important than ever to be able to fight back. Wildfires are dangerous and pose great risks. Thankfully, firefighters and scientists have many tried-and-true, as well as new, methods and technology to deal with them.

Making a Firebreak

The aim of all firefighting is to take away from the blaze of one of the three ingredients of fire that it needs to grow—fuel, oxygen, or heat. Firebreaks rob blazes of fuel. A firebreak is a strip of land around a fire that is cleared of dry plants and plant waste. To create a firebreak, firefighters carefully burn the fuel load or use bulldozers to clear the ground. They may even use axes, rakes, or other tools to remove trees and dig up plants in some places. When the fire reaches that point, it has nothing to feed on. It should then die out.

Firefighters risk their lives to get up close to fires in order to create firebreaks.

Flying Fire Fighting

Special aircraft called air tankers are used to fly over a fire and drop large amounts of water onto the flames. That cools down the fire, robbing it of the heat that it needs to grow. Air tankers may also be used to drop fire retardants onto a blaze. Fire retardants are chemicals that slow or stop things burning by cooling them and blocking the oxygen that fires feed on. In some places, firefighters use drones to survey an area of fire. They also use special pilotless air tankers to drop fire retardant onto wildfires, which allows firefighters to keep their distance from the flames. Those techniques save firefighters' lives.

Large air tankers can be used to drop fire retardant over a wildfire. The retardant smothers the wildfire.

FRONT LINE GEAR

Firefighters wear specialized equipment that keeps them safe when they are firefighting on the front line. They wear masks to help them breathe and prevent them from breathing in smoke. They wear clothing made from a fireproof material to protect them from the intense heat. They may also carry special tents, called fire shelters. They can be put up in an instant to protect the firefighters from extreme heat if they become trapped in a fire.

Disaster Zone

California

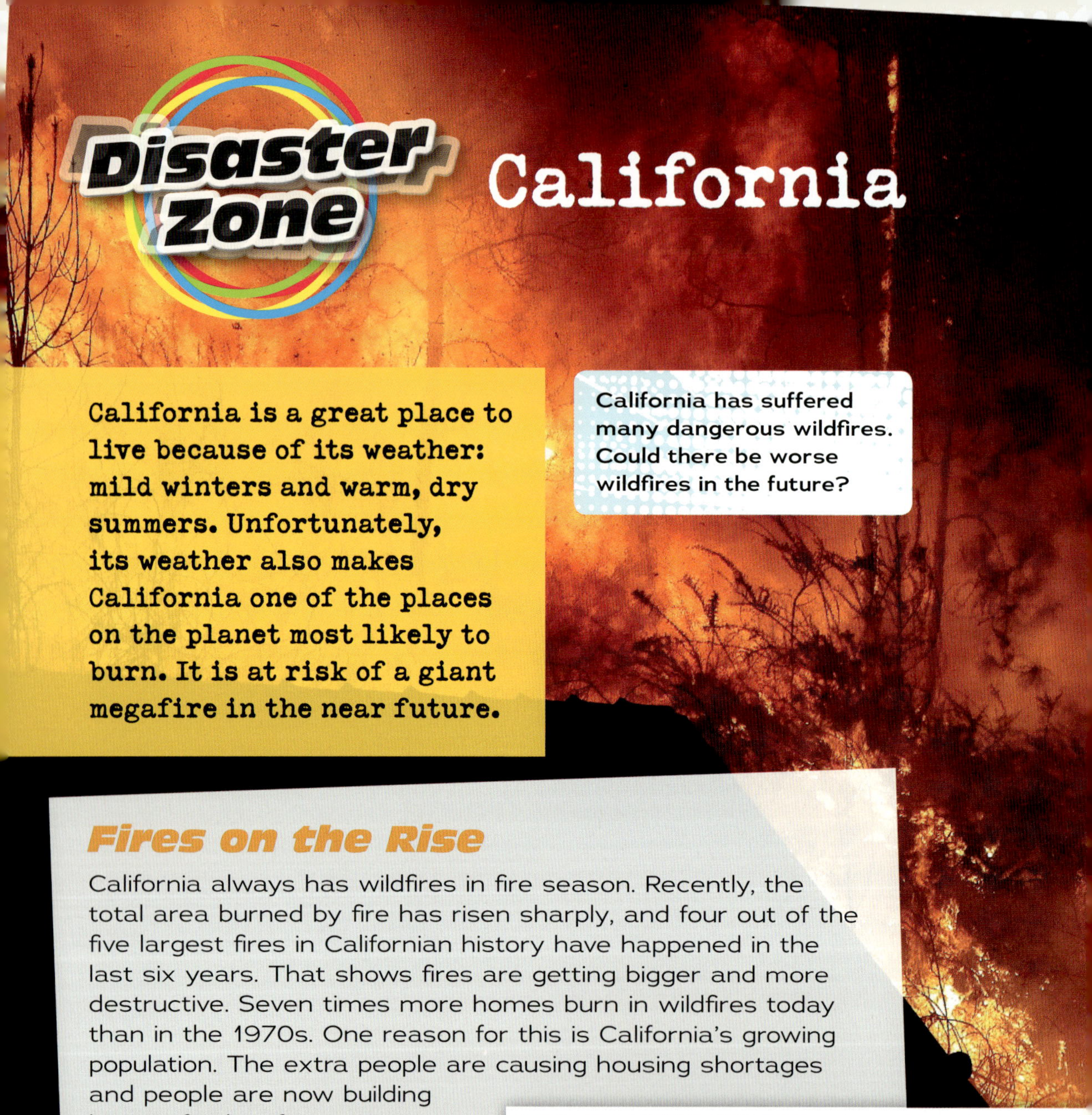

California is a great place to live because of its weather: mild winters and warm, dry summers. Unfortunately, its weather also makes California one of the places on the planet most likely to burn. It is at risk of a giant megafire in the near future.

California has suffered many dangerous wildfires. Could there be worse wildfires in the future?

Fires on the Rise

California always has wildfires in fire season. Recently, the total area burned by fire has risen sharply, and four out of the five largest fires in Californian history have happened in the last six years. That shows fires are getting bigger and more destructive. Seven times more homes burn in wildfires today than in the 1970s. One reason for this is California's growing population. The extra people are causing housing shortages and people are now building homes farther from city centers and closer to wild places. When fires happen, they are most at risk.

The bigger the wildfire, the greater the danger that flames, heat, and smoke from the blaze will reach towns and cities in the area.

Fires in the Future

Future megafires could be disastrous. As wildfires move into populated areas, entire cities could be wiped out. Fire will destroy more animals and wildlife habitat. More smoke and ash will fill the air and linger for weeks. People will breathe in more dangerous particulate matter. Some people fear that the cost of **insuring** homes will rise. Insurance will become too expensive for many people to afford to buy it. If their homes burn down in a fire, they will have no chance of rebuilding them.

FIRES ON THE RISE

In the 1970s, approximately 3 million acres (1.2 million ha) of land burned in the United States in an average year. Between 2000 and 2010, that figure was more than 7 million acres (2.8 million ha). Before 1995, the United States had on average fewer than one megafire per year. Between 2005 and 2014, there was an average of 9.8 megafires per year.

Chapter 6

BE PREPARED

There is no doubt that wildfires will happen in the future. They can occur wherever it is warm, dry, and windy, with high plant fuel loads. People in those areas must prepare for wildfires to protect themselves.

Forest Management

An important part of fire prevention is managing forests. Cutting down dead, drying branches from trees helps reduce fire size. Dead wood catches fire more easily than living wood, which is moist. It helps to cut out branches that overlap between trees. Removing climbing plants such as vines and ivy increases the space between tree crowns, which reduces crown fires. Sometimes, firefighters let small natural wildfires burn. They burn away dead trees, small plants, and plant waste that could add to future fuel loads.

Safety at Home

People can reduce damage from wildfires by making buildings less likely to burn. Wooden buildings can be treated with fire-resistant sprays. It also helps to build a large source of water near a house, such as a swimming pool. In an emergency, it can be used to put out flames. It is also important to create a fire-resistant zone around homes. That is an area that is free of leaves, plant waste, or other flammable materials. People could also plant trees such as oaks rather than coniferous trees. Oaks are less likely to burn and spread fires that could reach homes.

Where in the World?

A wildfire swept through 2,000 acres (810 ha) in the hills north of San Diego, California, in May 2014. Houses in one area were burned to the ground, while others nearby escaped unharmed. Why did that happen? Many of the homes that survived had very little flammable brush in the area immediately around them. The other homes had dry grass and shrubs close by. Gutters were filled with pine needles, and trash cans left open against a wall. In the end, it was the little things that made a difference.

Using controlled, smaller fires that can be easily put out robs wildfires of the fuel they need to spread.

Removing flammable material such as dead, dry leaves from around a house can reduce the risk of it catching fire in a wildfire.

WILDFIRE WARNINGS

When a wildfire happens, it is important to act immediately. People should listen for warnings during fire seasons. They must make sure everyone in their family knows what a warning sounds like, and everyone should know what to do when one is given.

In 2009, California's Station Fire was the largest wildfire of the season and warnings went off the charts.

How Warnings Work

Warnings about possible fires are given on the radio, television, and Internet broadcasts. The national weather service announces them. Warnings are given when weather conditions are right for fire. That means high temperatures, low moisture levels, and high winds. There are different types or levels of warning. For example, in the United States, a Fire Weather Watch means there might be severe fire weather in the next 12 to 24 hours. A Red Flag Warning says that conditions are right for fires to start and existing fires to quickly spread.

Q

How do you think schools can help educate students about preparing for a wildfire? What measures could they put in place?

Taking Action

It is essential to have a family emergency plan in wildfire-prone regions. That should include a plan for how to escape a house if it catches fire. It should also include which escape routes to follow to get to a safe place, such as open playing fields or coastline. It is best to figure out several different ways to leave the area and get to safety because some routes might be cut off by fire. Before leaving home, people should turn off their gas supply. They should put their pets in the car ready to go with them, if there is enough time. A fire could happen when family members are all in different places, such as school and work. So people should make a plan for where to meet up, or ways to get in touch if they are separated.

BEING PREPARED

People in wildfire-prone zones need to keep a disaster supply kit or emergency kit ready for fire season. The kits include items such as a radio to hear fire news, and food and water. A first aid kit, a flashlight with spare batteries, and breathing masks should go in the kit. It should also include fire service and emergency numbers.

Candles, matches, and a few cans of food can be useful additions to an emergency kit in the event of a fire.

SURVIVING A RAGING WILDFIRE

Raging wildfires are awesome forces of nature and they will continue into the future. Reading and learning about wildfires helps us know what to do before and when one happens. It helps people survive.

Keeping Safe

Knowing how to spot the early signs of a wildfire can save lives. Although a raging wildfire can move quickly, there are sometimes warning signs. Warning signs could include rising smoke or even flames from a faraway section of forest or prairie. Another early sign is the faint smell of wood smoke. The sight of a thin coating of ash on nearby surfaces caused by small, smoldering fires is another sign. Early signs of smoke can be a hazy sky. Large wildfires also make a lot of noise—wood will crack and tall trees crash to the ground. If people spot these signs, they should check the radio for warnings, and should go in the opposite direction of the fire as quickly as possible.

The haze of smoke from wildfires can be a warning sign that people should **evacuate** an area.

During a wildfire, people should know to gather at an evacuation control center to escape the fire.

Hope for the Future

Raging wildfires can be very dangerous, and the thought of seeing or experiencing one can be very scary. While it is important to take wildfires seriously, it helps to remember that people can do a lot to protect themselves from those fires. If they take precautions and listen to and obey evacuation warnings, they should be safe. Experts are always working on ways to reduce fire risks. They study how to better control them when they happen, and how to give people plenty of warning so they can get out of the way of the frightening flames.

SPEND NOW, SAVE LATER

Today. many experts argue that more money should be spent on managing areas where wildfires are likely to help prevent them from taking place. They say that the cost of repairing the damage caused by a future megafire will be far greater than the cost of spending now to keep fire-prone places under control. As wildfires increase, it is an argument that is becoming harder to ignore.

Glossary

atmosphere the blanket of gases that surrounds Earth
brush an area of rough open land covered with bushes and trees
bushfires fires in wild, shrubby land, often in Australia
charred blackened by being partly burned
chemical reaction a process in which substances are converted into different substances
climates the regular patterns of weather in a place
crops plants grown for food
current a river of moving water within the ocean
debris pieces from something that has been destroyed
deforestation the process of cutting down or burning large areas of forest
drones unmanned robotic aircraft
embers small pieces of burning or glowing wood
energy the strength needed for activity
environment the natural world around us
equator an imaginary horizontal line around the middle of Earth, dividing it in half
evacuate to move away from danger in an organized way
evaporates turns from a liquid into a gas
extinction the complete dying out of a species
fertile good for growing plants
flammable easily set on fire
fossil fuels oil, coal, and gas formed from long-dead plants and animals
fuel a material that burns
grassland open land on which many types of grasses grow
grazing slowly feeding on plants
habitat the place in which an animal or plant lives
humidity the amount of moisture in the air
insuring making regular payments to a company, which will then pay for any damage or loss
livestock farm animals
monsoon heavy seasonal rain
original the first of something
oxygen a gas found in the air and needed for breathing
particles tiny pieces of something
particulate matter tiny pieces of materials that float in the air
prairie open land in North America on which a lot of grasses grow
predators animals that hunt and eat other animals for food
rain forests areas of thick forests where there is regular heavy rainfall
remote far away from towns and cities
satellite a human-made object that orbits, or circles, Earth
sensors devices that detect, and send information about, properties such as heat, sound, or light
tropical describes the hot region near Earth's equator
unpredictable likely to change suddenly and without warning

Find Out More

Books

Brundle, Joanna. *Heat Waves and Wildfires* (Transforming Earth's Geography). KidHaven Publishing, 2019.

Gagliardi, Sue. *California Wildfires* (21st Century Disasters). North Star Editions, 2019.

London, Martha. *Wildfires* (Extreme Weather). DiscoverRoo, 2019.

Siegel, Rachel. *California and Other Western Wildfires* (Disaster Alert!). Crabtree Publishing, 2018.

Websites

Learn more about wildfires at:
www.nationalgeographic.com/environment/natural-disasters/wildfires

Find factsheets about wildfires at:
www.nfpa.org/public-education/by-topic/wildfire

Discover what to do when a wildfire happens at:
www.ready.gov/wildfires

Publisher's note to educators and parents:
All the websites featured above have been carefully reviewed to ensure that they are suitable for students. However, many websites change often, and we cannot guarantee that a site's future contents will continue to meet our high standards of educational value. Please be advised that students should be closely monitored whenever they access the Internet.

Index

About the Author

Louise Spilsbury is an award-winning author who has written hundreds of wonderful books for children. She has written many books about natural disasters and has a healthy respect for these awesome forces of nature!